Obscura

Obscura

POEMS BY
FRANK PAINO

ORISON
BOOKS

ISBN: 978-1-949039-07-8

Orison Books
PO Box 8385
Asheville, NC 28814
www.orisonbooks.com

Distributed to the trade by Itasca Books
1-800-901-3480 / orders@itascabooks.com

Cover photo by Gerrie Paino of the sculpture "Eternal Silence" by
Lorado Taft, Graceland Cemetery, Chicago.

Manufactured in the U.S.A.

ORISON
BOOKS

CONTENTS

FOREWORD

Nickole Brown

The only good thing about being called for jury duty some twenty years ago was that cell phones were smart enough to still be only phones and the courthouse (at least in my city) didn't have anything resembling wireless, which meant I got a full week's reprieve from office emails and the opportunity to catch up on personal reading. One volume I lugged along for the feast was *The Face of Poetry*, a hefty anthology edited by Zack Rogow that featured many known stars, from Ashbery to Kinnell, and I enjoyed myself well enough until I neared the end of the book and something stopped me cold—a piece called "Each Bone of the Body," written by a poet I'd never heard of.

Accurately introduced as a work that links religious imagery and sensuality "in a way that heightens both, till the poem rises to a fevered temperature," this poem was unlike anything I'd experienced before. Within those lines, I stepped from that dreary waiting room into a gothic cathedral made of words, its architecture intricately baroque and deeply mournful—all of it haunted by a kind of chiaroscuro that depicted the despair of "the six o'clock news" as a darkness made darker still, lit as it was in contrast to the intense but ephemeral flame of human desire. Now, I had heard Emily Dickinson's dictum enough times to think it cliché, but there I was, feeling as if the top of my head were taken off, quite physically, right there among a room full of bored and restless jurors. And yes, I knew: it was poetry, the real kind that keeps you reading for years until you find it again.

The poem was by Frank Paino. At that time, he hadn't published in nearly ten years, but I did my immediate best to read everything by him I could find. After spending weeks immersed in that otherworldly spell only his poems cast, I decided to track him down. I worked in independent publishing then and wanted to see if he had a manuscript he could submit. Frank replied that he didn't have enough material for a book, but we did strike up a correspondence, first sending emails back and forth, mostly about the challenges of the writing life, then eventually moving on to compose and send letters the old-fashioned way—handwritten and slow enough in response to deeply consider the most important things.

Ten years on, this exchange is one of the most vital in my life, despite the fact that now I'm on the road long enough not to be able to get to my mailbox for weeks, which is where I likely was when my friend, Luke Hankins, the founder and publisher of Orison Books—who often is kind enough to stay at the house while my wife Jessica Jacobs and I travel—spotted Frank's two books on our poetry shelves (or more accurately, all four copies of Frank's two books, as both my wife and I refused to give up our individual personal copies when we married and then slowly melded our libraries). It was a coincidence without any prompting from me, but it's no surprise that Luke immediately recognized the startling power of Frank's poems, and just as I did all those years ago, contacted him in hopes he might send his pages along to Orison.

This is all to say that here, in your hands, is the result of nearly twenty years of things that were meant to be. And should you believe in that tricky bit of business done by the Fates themselves, you should thank those wily sisters. With all of the lush but haunted eroticism of his previous work, Frank moves away from personal narrative to investigate the lives (and more often the deaths) of others in this long-awaited third collection that weaves a tapestry as macabre as it is achingly sorrowful. This work, with a fetish-like attention to detail, enters the chambers of history we often avoid, stepping into skins both human and beast. With an unflinching eye, these poems peer into glass coffins, formaldehyde-filled jars, and photographs of horrific scenes—they crouch among the dank silence of catacombs and reliquaries and ruins—all to hear what the dead might have to say.

At times, the brutalization depicted makes for a deeply uneasy read, but always the victims of such violence are beautified and beatified, canonized in the way perhaps only an artist can. Ultimately, Frank's fascinations sift the wreckage out of grief, desperate to find a way we can all rightly live with so much loss. Because, reader, be warned: within these pages is no typical lyric meditation on how our bodies are destroyed or what becomes of them after their end. No, this is a book unlike anything else being written today. You won't be likely to forget what you encounter here. To quote Frank's description of an exquisitely beautiful photograph of a suicide victim who fell to her death: Once you've seen it, you'll be "powerless to turn away."

for Gerrie, again

. . . tell us all the bad things
beauty's made of.

           –**Danusha Laméris**

Or did you mean to ask
"Why are you sad so often?"

Ask the moon.
Ask what it has witnessed.

           –**Linda Pastan**

The End of All Flight

The first bird was a serpent,
green in a tree that dripped
apples red as an opened vein,
though death, at that time,
was only a rumor the blades
of sawgrass whispered
when combed
by the wind's shrill fingers.

The first bird was a serpent
with wings, whom Eve beheld
during love's first exhalation
as she raked Adam's gleaming
breast, the scar
where he'd been stitched back
together a scythe that already cut
distance between them.
The first bird's speech was
pure sibilance.
Its language was desire.

The second bird was a god,
was a swan
whose truth was brutal,
though stone and canvas refused
to tell how its great wings were
flecked with the mud and slime
it forced the woman into,
its breath foul with dead fish,
rough skin dotted
with mites that scoured the scales
caught in its tattered plumage.

The second bird was a god
who plunged through stuttering air

as frightened swans rose
from the pungent riverbank.

The third bird was a dove,
was a spirit
who spoke in tongues
of fire that made a young girl
believe it was love
that broke open the clenched
fist inside her
and love that would smooth
the seam back toward innocence.

The third bird was a dove
with a poison-tipped beak
it used like a nail, a nib
touched to a radiant double helix
that became a living word
within her. Though even that
word was a lie, no different
from any that had gone before—
apple, swan, son of man—
the end of all flight is a falling.

Cephalophores

I must have been twelve
the first time I heard it—
cephalophore . . .
the word vaguely phallic
on the tongue of the young nun
I'd fallen in love with,
the one who introduced us
to the host of decapitated
saints who lifted their severed heads
from the blood-gorged ground
and walked—sometimes for miles,
sometimes singing—
until they finally lay down
forever, faces cradled
in the cups of their upturned palms.

So many someone invented a word for them.
So many you don't have to look
hard to find one fracturing
light into bright rainbows
high in an old church window or
standing on a pedestal,
grisly freight held up
like a child's first lost tooth.

Here, a bishop hoists his head
heavenward by the fish-mouth
of his scarlet mitre. Here, the calm
countenance of a young girl floats
like an unleashed dog
just ahead of her strolling corpse.

One ravishing saint, nude
but modest beneath the drapery
of her extravagant locks, ·

thrusts the macabre lantern
of her lustrous face
into the hoop of darkness
formed by the retreating mob.

For some, the nimbus burns
a hole into the absence
just above the severed throat,
while others bear the light
in polished golden rings
that circle the drifting brow.

As a child, they haunted my
thunderstorm nights, slouching
in black hollows, harrowing
the foot of my bed
where they'd cast terrible,
truncated shadows
across the coverlet
when lightning tore the sky
in jagged, gunmetal seams.

Four decades beyond
my childish fears,
the headless still keep me awake
some nights, though nowadays
they appear as unwilling martyrs
of gods and governments,
men and women who kneel
in sad rooms
halfway around the world,
their grainy, televised faces
turning from sharp fate,
and, having undergone
such rough divorce,
give the lie to pious fantasies.
They cannot stoop to lift
all they have lost and bear it

to some marvelous conclusion.

Sleepless now, I long for
those faraway fears.
What wouldn't I do to conjure
the cephalophores
to lie with me upon this shroud
of twisted bedsheets
and become again
my deepest dread?
I would hold their heads
in my tremulous hands,
kiss the ice–blue
mouths of the haloed dead,
their lips tasting of
copper and communion wine.
I would let their blood pool
upon my pillow
in the spilt moonlight.
I would let them
do as they wished with me.
Whatever it might take.
Anything. Anything at all.

If There Is Such a Thing as Mercy

Martha, last passenger pigeon, 1885–1914

In that cage of the already-ghost,
indecorous in your molt and dotage,
unable to ascend more than the half-hop
it took to mount the rough wooden perch
where days passed in the tremulous wake
of apoplexy, where thoughtless visitors tossed
handfuls of sand to stir you from your torpor,
in that cage of the billion-to-one,
if there was such a thing as mercy,
perhaps it descended in dreams drenched
in genetic memory, where the crowd's cacophony
transmuted to the mother tongue
of your vanished dynasty whose chatter once buried
the black thunder of a dozen locomotives,
whose passing overhead could evict daylight,
routing the horizon like a smoke-grey shroud
swept over the sun.

But that was before a century of settlers came,
insatiable for food and sport and the cruel amusement
of boys with rakes heaved through the feathered flurry,
before a single round of buckshot would tumble
a dozen or more from the wing-thick cloud
without the trouble of taking aim,
before poisoned corn was flung across fallow fields
and sulfur burned to choke back each last breath
year upon wheeling year until the skytrails dwindled
from days, to hours, to a swift afterthought
above the tree line and, finally, only you, a single,
flightless female left to mark the diminishing days

of your bloodline in a barren Cincinnati zoo.

And after they found you unyielding and still
in the bottom of your cage, came the indignities
of ice and scrutiny, of scalpels to release your bowels
and the alchemist's exquisite taxidermy
that brought you back to strange half-life,
poised on a slender branch to keep, forever,
your solitary watch.
Bird of what lies in ruins.
Bird of a billion-to-none.
Bird of a lesson we refuse to learn.

The Drowned Church of Potosí, Venezuela

*In 1985, the town of Potosí was deliberately flooded
to create a reservoir for a hydroelectric power plant.*

The citizens are all gone to higher ground,
having gathered what's essential and left the rest

to breathlessness. Nothing remains but to watch
as the dammed river backs into the valley

to await its churning rebirth into light.
Let the elements exchange their mantles,

fertile jade for an unquiet umber that will,
in time, settle to a blue-green equilibrium.

But for now, a quiet chaos as arched doorways,
tiled roofs, acquiesce to the insistent stroke

of unnatural tide. Evenings, after the children have been
put down in unfamiliar beds, the women gather to weep,

share visions of the catacombs beneath the church
backfilled with the heft of all that was left behind.

Here, a cache of frankincense sifts down
like amber snowfall. Here, a table too frail to endure

such rough exodus catches in the corridors of the dead,
who, for their part, turn and rattle against the stones.

The displaced mothers speak of worn wooden pews

that once cradled them, bearing now the weight

of silt and plunging shadow. The scarlet curtains
that muffled their sins drift like veils of wanton brides,

while the carved altar with its relic stone flashes white
in deepening currents that lick the chiseled thighs

of the man who hangs lifeless on a cross too heavy
to shoulder into the mountain's anoxic atmosphere.

Soon, the silken hair that adorns his head will lift,
then tangle, in the thorns that weave his crown.

Soon, the ribbed vault of ceiling that once called back
a host of hymns will echo only the distant whine

of turbines past the penstock, the buzz of outboards
carrying the curious above the ruins.

Rain and rain. The terrible hulk of water setting
a new high mark each hour. On the final night,

the refugees gather against a clamoring storm,
pull capes close as the swollen reservoir hoists itself up

toward the tower's cross-tipped steeple
where the tongue of the ancient bell hangs

mute as its throat begins to close, though the women swear
one solitary toll thunders from the rising black,

as if to beckon a cold-blooded congregation to enter
and praise the power that is descending.

Mercy

For weeks he has watched the still heart
of the sails, prayed for unseen breath
to lift canvas from the riggings.
He has prayed for a deck baptized with spume
and the quicksilver bellies of fishes.
But the ocean refuses to shrug, offers only
August sun back to itself without blemish.

These days, fortune is measured in half-ladles
of fresh water, the pitted rind of an orange,
flayed skin of a withered apple.

In the hold beneath him, hulks of draped
crates haunt the air with the odor of saffron
and unspent Spanish gold too heavy for the spindly
arms of his crew to heave overboard.

He asks himself what more he might do,
and in answer turns his gaze to the place
where the horses have been gathered.
No munitions to spare. No strength or stomach
for bloodletting. No choice he can see
but the terrible leagues of breathless blue.

Unashamed, he wipes the sting from his eyes,
ties a kerchief around the sharp angles
of his favorite mare's head,
closing her view of endlessness,
seeing, as he performs this small mercy,
a rime of dried sweat circling the moss of her
flared nostrils as she buries her muzzle
in the barley cupped in his outstretched palm
and follows him toward the cerulean gape,
her chestnut flanks rising and falling like tidewater.

And now a slap on her croup, hard enough
to make her start, fetlocks fraying in flight
as if she means to tread sheer atmosphere,
then a black hoof brands a slick half-moon
above his heart a moment before she vanishes
in a sickle of sunlight and salt spray only to break
the surface a moment after, blowing the great trumpets
of her lungs, the blindfold torn loose and floating free.

And now the panic of sixty more hooves
driven forward by rough hands,
water churning sorrel, bay, dappled grey,
until pink veins of blood from brine-singed
throats stain the sea like a tincture.

A handful of sailors crack oars against thrashing legs
to hasten the drowning, though it will be hours
before the last of them stops knocking the keel,
each strike like a heartbeat . . . or the tongue
of a bell in its diminishing arc.

Hell's Gate

"They tell me I was down in the tomb an hour and a half.
That must be a mistake. I was down there a year."
**–Charles P. Everett, bell diver who explored the sunken
steamer,** *General Slocum*, **16 June 1904**

Fire, yes. But first there was water
and early summer sky, an unblemished blue
offered back to itself as if from a mirror's
reliable surface. Onboard—music,
bright confections, and the liquid-silver refrains
of laughter. Then something soft as
the sound wings make as they lift,
then pull towards light. The swift sizzle
of a match spark on the hay-tindered floor
of the forward hold—heavy hinges swung
toward the hasp, sealing everything poised
that side of regret in breathlessness—
which might have choked on its own ill intent
were it not for the deckhand who threw back
the hatch, fed that infernal blossom
just as the ship's great wheels churned
into Hell's Gate, thick with white-knuckle waves,
the sinister suck of whirlpools, and the clutch
of swift currents just a hand's-breadth beneath.

Unaware, the passengers danced until
the floorboards began to bow and blister,
the band's music halted, the dance itself
not stopped, but transformed
into something macabre, five-hundred
spinning skirts and wide sleeves flaring white to
black through a toll of ochre, almost chartreuse at
its core, while the captain steamed upwind

toward North Brother Island, fresh paint and bunting
shedding a shawl of blood-orange in its wake,
the *Slocum* itself, one plumed, searing torch,
open decks flooded with men and women
who clasped their sons and daughters
or tore at each other, their choice—fire or water—
the means through which each would rise
or fall into eternity.

One-thousand twenty-one souls.
And few who could swim. And few who could
tread water or fight the rotted cork jackets
as they filled with East River tide
that pulled them down like anchor chains
past the light's myopic reach.

Twenty minutes and most of the dying
was over, the steamer impaled on mossy rock
in shallows too deep for wading.
On shore, nurses and patients spilled
from the doors and lower casements
of the island's quarantine, bearing ladders,
spools of gauze, and clean linens,
a froth of white that rushed down past
the sea wall where the *Slocum*'s hulk smoldered
at a starboard list—hundreds still held within
that timber tomb—while above their quiet forms
eddies stirred the drifting dead, unpinned tangled
tresses to traceries. And the white blooms
of petticoats, bonnets, child-sized blankets, opened
against the liquid blue, as if a throng of revelers
had just passed through the gates of hell,
casting handfuls of pale roses as they went.

Descent

Harriet Westbrook Shelley, 1816

Early December and the moon bloats with milky light.
Hyde Park sleeps, silvered in ice that wraps the naked elms,
the lampposts and curved benches. Inside her, heaviness
thick as the silt and mud on the Serpentine's bottom.
What creatures, she wonders, burrow in that cold silence
through winter, or wait, still as held breath, for a death
that moves, cell by gilded cell, toward each purple, thickening heart?

She thinks there must be bliss in such surrender,
cradled in a hush of fallen leaves, the dull shimmer of fish scales
like faraway stars, each thing transmuted but sustained.
She knows bliss is mindless, unconscious of what possesses it—
a lesson learned at Shelley's side, through pewter clouds of opium smoke,
the two of them pressed hip to hip, lungs swollen
with oblivion's heavy breath. And will the weight of water
be the same as it opens inside her?

It is the memory of that sweet forgetfulness which has brought her
to this moment just past sunset, the hem of the ivory dress
soon to be her shroud caught on the unpolished balustrade
as she stands on the bridge lip's slight declension. She thinks about
the soldier she met in June, how in his fumbling rush he'd only partially
disrobed. And the sound his medals made—like faint applause—
when his body shuddered above her.

Later came the queasy, seasick mornings, the dark, almost bruised
areolar blush. And now the flutter and kick of the small swimmer
beneath her belly's dome. This secret she can no longer keep.
She pauses, not from fear but from desire, holds her breath in
and then, in, to build a greed deep in her lungs so they will not refuse
the water's cold intrusion. One moment. One last intake of breath
on its slender plume, and then a simple

stepping off

the blue of her chenille walking shoes going black in the water's wick.
A hoop of ivory skirting, brief air trapped in the swell. Then the darkening
velvet belt, swollen breasts, shoulders, corded throat, the delicate loveliness
of her face going under, mouth open—swallowing new atmosphere.

Frigid. Mindless. The Serpentine pours through blood-thick lungs,
the shocked and clamoring heart. When she goes still, that other heart,
being no stranger to water, thrums a few moments more, though soon enough
the silk-thin veins will carry only what is vacuous, as may be the bulk of any bliss.

Falling

On 27 September 1827, William Forsyth of the Pavilion Hotel, Niagara Falls, chained live animals to a schooner and sent them over the cataract as a means of attracting tourists to his establishment.

What if the buffalo, fur matted with mud and dung,
had tucked one glass-slick horn beneath the ribs
of the man who led him aboard the decommissioned
schooner, her two masts jutting into autumn sky
as she scraped the wooden dock a mile or so up the Niagara
where the Horseshoe's thunder seemed more like
the thrum of honeybees?

What if the raccoon had dragged its rabid teeth
along the pale flesh of its handler's wrist, a surgical slice
just above the glove-line he would shrug off
until night fell with its fever and slow asphyxiation?

What if the lioness, halt in her dotage but still mad
for life, had clawed a mortal gape into her captor's jugular,
leaving him to bleed out across the bleached fir decking?

Or what if the three she bears had made of their claws
a crown of thorns to tear open the scalp of William Forsyth,
baring the skull of the hotelier who dreamed
the marvel of "ferocious beasts" swallowed by the cataract
would fill the rooms that stood, too-often, empty?

What if and what if.

But there is no such happy ending: there are only
15,000 revelers gathered at the end of September 1827
to watch this "reverse Noah's ark" carry her startled
freight over the lip of eternity. Only the well-dressed
young men, polished brass keys to the finest hotels

warm in breast pockets, the gloved hands of flushed brides
looped through their arms. Only fine leather shoes
and long skirts going dark where they brush wet pavement,
all eyes turned toward *The Michigan* as she floats into view
from Flat Rock, her rusted rails lined with the absurd forms
of burlap pirates lashed tight and unmoving,
though it is the wild-eyed animals, already drenched
from the tossing, that draw the crowds' attention,
harsh cries swallowed by the Roman coliseum roar
of water and men who lean hard out over the ledge
to better see the spectacle.

How they cheer as the keel screams over upthrust
boulders, sending a silver fox into white turbulence
where he disappears into his airless fate, and then
the ship herself, torn beneath the waterline
but sound enough to answer the current's incessant
call until the moment she is buoyed only by air,
water sluicing from ripped timbers, what creatures
remain held by chains or terror one last, uncountable
moment before ship and beasts drop through
the rippling curtain and break upon the rocks below.

The breathless crowd will stay a while longer, search
for any sign of life under the faded rainbow mist.
They'll watch a few splintered planks breach the foamed
surface and drift placidly away, then they'll stroll
to posh hotels where they'll dine in candlelight and relive
the day's distraction, each man boasting the very best view
while the women lie about deep swoons or how they
had to turn away. Later still, they'll retire to gas-lit rooms
where the sheets are strewn with roses and they'll fuck
with rough abandon, then fall asleep with windows
thrown full open to the water's lullaby. All night they'll
dream of hands that lift them in a kind of halting flight,
a lightness that slowly takes on dead weight, the way a dress
or winter jacket pulls a swimmer down—a tug that will
at last give way to a terrible, ceaseless, falling.

Plunder

*You are cordially invited to Lord Wellesley's (at Windermere) 5PM for
dinner & cocktails. Unwrapping of a mummy from Thebes to follow.*
–Victorian mummy unwrapping party invitation

Sulfur flares from match tips,
burns blue as Egyptian amulets
at the candle wicks, then rises,
burnished as the rays that snake
from a pharaoh's painted headdress.

Early evening. Sun slants
across wide lawns and summer gardens,
though here in this narrow room
the brocade curtains have been
drawn to beckon midnight.

At the table's furthest corner,
discarded dinner plates give off
a hint of sage and fowl, though where
the women gather it is the scent of amber resin,
juniper, and palm wine that rises,
sweet and primitive as lust.

Their breath is lean from tight-drawn
corsets and the kind of heady fear
they knew when the hard bodies of men
who entered them were still a novelty.

Blunt and grey against whorls
of buffed mahogany, their guest waits—
breathless, too—unmoved, even as
one woman pinches the cloth at his throat,
gently lifts it toward her lips
and then away, though too soon

she holds nothing more than powder
like a moth's wing brushed
against a velvet collar, and with
a grudging sigh she steps away
to wait another turn.

Some nights bring talismans
untucked from tight-wound linen,
papyri inked with hieroglyphs, or a purse
of precious gems the finder will stroke
with pale, gloved hands, then set aside
as if it were a tawdry favor.

Some nights the short arm
on the mantel clock unravels
painstaking hours of this undoing,
finger by wizened finger, limb by limb.
Others, a slim shadow slips over
only a few minute lines before the game
is over—before the mummy lies
wholly unveiled, black as delta mud
and hollow—or perhaps it crumbles
to biblical dust the maids will sweep into
crumb trays and trash bins come morning.

Silence and a laugh.
Silence and a shiver.

Ringed around the table,
the women stare and murmur,
unbinding what centuries held bound
with the disregard of children
who know only their own pleasure,
while the men ease back in leather
chairs, drowsed by deep draughts of
laudanum and slow dreams
of the night's inevitable conclusion…
how their lovers, having leaned so near

death they could kiss it, will regard
themselves in gilded mirrors
after warm, oiled baths, ivory brushes
sparking through hair unloosed
in the predawn dark, then step
from the embrace of fine silk robes
to lie on perfumed bedsheets.
They will open themselves
like long-hidden tombs that glisten
and beckon for plunder.

Until the End of the World

Dom Pedro & Inês de Castro
Alcobaça Monastery, Portugal

After the assassins' hearts are torn from them,
        after the new king feels their blood sluice

down his throat like a benediction of copper
        and fire, he lays aside his crown, bends to kiss

the unmoving mouth of his queen, whose brocade
        hem lifts like that of a shy girl or an early

summer morning to expose one fragile ankle
        looped three times with gold. Crowned and

jewel-laden, her veiled head appears to float above
        a coronation gown beaded with the yellow

wax of fragrant candles clutched in the unsettled
        hands of altar boys. Her lips, frozen

in a two-year rictus that might be pain or
        aching pleasure, open onto a toothless black

beneath which lies the greater blackness of
        her gaping throat. After so long a separation

that first kiss is like swallowing light,
        the way he'd once sworn he could taste

the sun in the purple flesh of a freshly plucked grape.
        Clutched in his hand is the rosary upon which

he has counted the days that have passed

and those that are to come, each bead offered

not to the Virgin but to the woman who was first
           his mistress and later his secret bride.

And though the gathered bishops turn in shame
           from Dom Pedro's sacrilege, they lurch forward

on his command, crimson mitres tucked beneath
           sweat-stained arms as they kneel to kiss the ring

that rattles against their new queen's stony finger,
           the air around her dark with the odor of earth-

worms and torn roots, though Dom Pedro seems to take
           no notice as he presses his mouth one final time

against her quiet lips, smooths the scarlet veil that falls
           like blood-thick water around her wasted shoulders.

And when, at last, he watches her marble likeness push
           shadows across the face that he adores, he scatters

the beads before the gilded altar and curses
           the god who hides behind two doors of beaten gold.

Six years later, Dom Pedro will lie down
           in death across from his bride so they may rest,

as the words he had inscribed upon his tomb proclaim,
           Until the end of the world, toe to marble

toe, their bejeweled heads like cardinal points
           on a mortal compass—his to the north, hers to the south—

defiantly turned from the promised Second Coming.
           What's left of love might be long as a femur or

brief as a handful of ash. On the day of resurrection,
        when flesh is once again woven over sinew and bone,

the wound in Inês' throat will be no more
        than a memory. The lovers will wake in darkness,

holding a first thought which was long ago their last.
        They will thrust aside the great weight

of their polished stones and open their eyes
        against sudden brightness

that will shimmer toward a vision of each other
        more divine than the sallow light descending

from the east to catch up those who put their faith
        in a love that finally saved them only from themselves.

Armageddon

It will start at the edge of the universe,
when the thrust of that ancient, unthinkable force,
finally spent, shudders to a halt in the airless dark.

Then, like a petulant child grown weary of sharing
gifts, it will begin to take everything back.
Stars, moons, entire scintillant galaxies will disappear
into the paradox that cradles in its emptiness
the rumor of all things.

Here on earth, generations will pass before we see
the nights grow a little darker with the turning years,
how each constellation's myth begins to change,
so that Orion's club is poised above some lesser beast
and the jeweled dippers are honed to demitasse,
until a time, far beyond any tomorrow we can know,
when the ghosts of our future wake to see light and dark
throw down their final hands.

On that day, each face will lift to watch the sun
tear off its robes of fire, setting the earth alight,
and in those last breathless seconds, we may finally
turn, each to the other, and forgive everything.

One moment, perfect as spring's first birdsong,
before that sudden paradise becomes
just another ember in a narrowing
throat of flame that ends
in starless
black.

Edison's Last Breath

A test tube on display at the Henry Ford museum allegedly contains Thomas Edison's last breath.

October, and the sycamore beyond the sheers bleeds
its green into the chill. Each leaf begins to glow
before its falling—a living filament—
though for him that light grows slender
the same way (how many years ago?)
sound began to taper until only lips pressed
to the softening ear could tear through the quiet
thick as the sweet butter Mina would spread
over the biscuits she brought for him each morning.

He reflects on what a twisted thing fate is—
or god—that he should finally be consumed
by an illness called Bright, kidneys flush
as febrile twins, uneasy in the cradle of his lower back.
And the slow burn, like a smoldering wick,
that draws a trickle of smoky urine, a shudder
flared from crown to toe, one jittery hitch of air
that makes his heart stutter like a thinning tungsten coil.

Edison turns back toward the chill pane's tracery,
its language of frost and light.
His eyes begin to glaze so that the world goes opaque
as a sheet of old glass, or the ghosts who drift
inside a mirror that's lost its silver.

When he wakes, the sun has gone a Tuscan gold
that glimmers just above the wooden sill.
He shifts beneath the downy coverlet,
feels the familiar froth of phlegm and blood
as it climbs the muscled ladder of his throat,
stains the white kerchief red as arils of pomegranate.

Slowly now, his chest begins to rise,
like a bowstring plucked by an archer's calloused fingers.
From a place just beneath the arc of his ribs
comes the first rasp of death's rattle.
And still, he cannot look away from the window,
from the tree with all its embers fanned
by unseen breeze, and the dim shape
of a rough-hewn door that cracks open
just beyond, spilling armfuls of scintillant light.

And now Mina is here, smelling of wood smoke
and apples. "It's very beautiful over there,"
he sighs as she brushes the damp from his brow,
sees a strange calm rise in his rheumy eyes
as he begins to slip off the tattered coat of his flesh.

And how might she restrain him?
He is unstoppable in his taking leave.
Already his absence begins to fill the room
like a vacuum. She knows no wretched photograph
nor knot of silvered hair can hold him fast
within a locket.

From a rack on the sill she plucks a slender vial,
holds it just above his pallid lips
until the glass begins to mist with his last sigh.

A seal of cork. A crust of paraffin.

She kisses his mouth one final time,
lifts the fragile prison up to the bedside lamp,
watches light pour through the settling fog
as it gathers itself in diminutive drops
like a thousand incandescent beads of polished glass.
His final, bright, benediction.

The Left Hand of the Devil

Niccolo Paganini, 1782–1840

Darkness. Fever moons on his gums wax,
mouth bandaged tight against death's gape.
To his left, a woman he cannot see
makes a sound that reminds him
of honeybees drugged by smoke but still hauling
their impossible plunder of sunlight.

Darkness and darkness. Click of rosary beads
like water on the forehead of a prisoner,
then a censer of frankincense to entice archangels
down from paradise, though it is the Devil's
feral wings that graze him, sharp as bull thistle
across open palms, strong enough to fill the pink sails
of his lungs, to pull him back from the stifling black,
make his boyish fingers flutter in the manner his father
had shown him, night after interminable night,
stroking the whorled neck of his violin until flesh
and wood became one seamless note upon another.

It takes him only two days to rise from the dead
though decades to ascend Europe's gas-lit stages,
face gaunt as the waning crescent moon,
his body's hunger for anything but music
an abomination as he forces one solitary string
to sing for the broken throats of its three lost sisters,
fingers stretched beyond mortal constraint,
his improbable perfection the thing that births
the legend behind his grand impenitence,
ashen face turned from the priest's white wafer
even as Death leans over the Battenberg pillow,

presses cold fingers to the knot in his throat
where cancer's taproot feeds its deadly flower.

Knowing what he does of winding sheets and shadow,
how can he do anything but stop his lips against
that diminutive moon? He will not offer himself to silence,
will not kneel before Death and swallow him whole.

Laika

First dog to be launched into low earth orbit.
Sputnik II, 3 November 1957

"Laika was quiet and charming . . . I wanted to do
something nice for her: She had so little time left to live."
–Dr. Vladimir Yazdovsky

Because she'd gone unbroken
by three years on Moscow's barren streets

she'd proved her will to survive simply
by surviving, and so was chosen

for a kind of brute salvation, a halfway gift
whose bad conclusion was already written

in a lack of funds and time and the keen
knowledge there'd be no way to bring her back.

And so began fierce weeks of acclimation:
each cage smaller than the last

to accustom her to stricture tight as
an overnight case,

the relentless gyre of the centrifuge
to mimic the weight of ascent,

and crude machines to simulate
the cacophonous dirge of ignition,

shrieking metal, everything it would take
to lift a thirteen-pound mongrel into history.

He called her Little Curly,
Little Bug. As if naming the doomed,

taking her home one night to play
with his two bright-eyed daughters,

could make the great burden of her
approaching death a lighter thing

to bend beneath when it came time to
tighten the harness just once again

and no more, to hold her in waiting
while the riddle of malfunction

was worked through its three-day resolution
and she watched from within

that aluminum tomb where she could stand
or lie but never turn, and late October's chill

settled its silver pall around her.
Three days and, finally, lift off.

Then, three anxious hours back on Earth
before they saw her heart's green tracery

slow again to nearly-calm
while the unshed core quietly kindled

its indigo fire inside the polished dome.
Listen, there is no other way to tell a thing

that has no mercy in it:
she burned up from the inside.

Fevered. Frantic. Blood-boiled.
Six-hundred miles between herself and

solid ground.
And there's no faith to be placed

in the weary myth of sacrifice;
no way to make right

the trust that was betrayed—
the muzzle and mad tongue of it—

how she was thrust into weightlessness,
into the useless memory of the man

who spoke softly, who turned,
at last, from the wild extravagance

of the round and riveted window
about which he'd been so adamant,

as if she might somehow savor
the breathless view, the spinning blue

that beckoned like a ball tossed into a street
she could only return to in flames.

Dog / Buddha

The air, just now, tinged
with jewelweed and the amber
talc of pollen. Lemon zest
of sunlight knifing off windshields.
Tang of wet wash drifting
on clotheslines. A brief burst
of bubblegum. Chalk on a sidewalk
where girls leap at hopscotch.
The metallic whiff
of a freshly-skinned knee.
Hydrangea. Cardiocrinum,
with its dangle of alabaster bells.
Cedar sap from a newly-set
fence. A dozen dinner scents
from summer's open windows.
Somewhere nearby something
has died. Already it begins
to dismantle in the breeze.
Laughter, stiletto shouts,
bicycle tires' hum on asphalt,
radio flare and the pesky munch
of a blood-bloated tick—
all caught in preposterous
flopping ears, bright wind-teared
eyes and the quivering black nose
that marks the farthest point
of that abandoned leaning
as the car accelerates—
sight, sound, taste, and feel—
everything as it is, just now.

52

"52" is the moniker given to an unidentified whale (most-likely a blue or fin) whose high-pitched vocalizations, at a frequency of 52hz, are unique among such mammals. Other whales do not respond to his calls, and this has led some to label him "The Loneliest Whale in the World."

Whether blue or fin or offspring of some uncommon union of each, I hope they never find you—that your song, smoothing its waves across oscilloscope screens from Kodiak Island to California's fractured coast, is never traced to the swirled wake of your singular breaches. Let the compassionate imagine you lonely, dream of soothing you in their sleek wetsuits and webbed gloves. Let the broken-hearted call you broken-hearted, too. And the ones who don't fit in, let them ink your slender lines along their biceps, needle your flukes across their backs like flightless wings. But let me conceive you beyond hapless solitude, beyond what's particular, unrequited, apart. Let me envision you a behemoth beyond betrayal, beyond desire for anything more than the titanic world through which you sail, your shadow longer than the broken-backed wrecks you pass over like some barnacled holy ghost. 52. Not even a name, just the frequency you sing at, a number driven belly-deep into your legend like a harpoon fired over the foam-flecked gunwales of a North Pacific whaler. 52. Swallower of messages sealed in bottles. Pack-mule for each grief or joy we make you bear. Monarch of misfits. Psalmist of an unknown tongue. May you drift beyond our seeing when gulls at last descend to lift your flesh in red mouthfuls—weightlessness of water exchanged for weightlessness of air.

The Burning of Giordano Bruno

Rome: 17 February 1600

"Perhaps you, my judges, pronounce this sentence against me with
greater fear than I receive it."
  **–Giordano Bruno, upon being sentenced to be burned at
  the stake for heresy**

They have driven a spike
through his palate.
As if holding his tongue
might stop the earth in its orbit.

They will set fire to the man
they held seven years
in a lightless cell,
the damp so heavy it numbered
his joints for the counting.

In the marketplace they have
stacked a pyre of sapwood,
green-skinned and rain-moist,
to slow the coming of his
last ragged breath.

The Inquisitors strip him,
chain his arms to the splintered
stake, then step back beneath
embroidered canopies
as the crowd puts torches
to tinder and begins to dance
for god's delight.

Giordano is unafraid.
These hard years have taught him
to drift beyond the shadow
of his flesh, observe the claws
and thumbscrews,
the rakes and studded racks
as if they tore only the body
of an uncanny effigy.

What matter, then, is fire?

He understands their blinkered faith,
their refusal to see
the universe is centered everywhere
without perimeter, and they,
spinning around the planet's
most brilliant star, are kindred
to infinite worlds beyond.

If he could part his lips,
he would proclaim it even now,
as the holy men thrust a silver crucifix
through the shivering wall
of smoke and cinder.

Bruno turns from that dying god
without regret. He has no use
for such brute salvation.
His hair lifts in the updraft,
transforms to fiery wings,
then disappears.
He feels his skin draw closer to bone.

Soon, there will be nothing.

Or, perhaps, something
he could never have supposed.

He gazes down on the gathered
throng: brightly-clothed
women and men—
here and there, a small boy
or girl—a glorious,
dancing host that moves
in tireless orbit around the light
he is becoming.

Caritas Romana

Say the sun dragged its shimmering nib over the dank stone floor
        through days he could no longer number.
Say his manacles drew blood like a demon's wedding band.
Say the rats grew corpulent on crusts tossed by the jailers
        while his ribs rose like the dead
           who stalked his unquiet dreams.

Say she steeled herself against the things she knew men would do
        to a woman who dared walk prison halls.
Say she closed her eyes. Say she endured.
Say, at last, she stooped to enter his solitary keep, unloosed
        the soft waves of her robe to the flush
           above her furious heart.

Say even a father could not refuse such tenderness.

Say the guards who found in her the secret vessel
        of his permanence could do nothing but grant mercy.
Say they stood back as she eased him
        through the crosshatched spills of sallow light.
Say each one in turn refused her gaze, fell silent
        as the tongues of temple bells past midnight.

Litany of "The Most Beautiful Suicide"

Empire State Building

Let her awaken unafraid
          on the first of May, 1947.
Let her put on her rose dress & makeup,
          her double-strand of pearls.
Let her check out
          of the Hotel Governor Clinton
          & walk east on 34th Street.
Let her enter the Empire's lobby
          with its strata of gold.
Let the ticket vendor take the coins
          from her white-gloved hand.
Let the elevator rise to the open deck
          on the 86th floor.
Let her lay down her purse
          & family photos.
Let her fold her long tan coat just so.
Let her offer her alabaster scarf
          to the mild mid-morning breeze.
Let her close her shadowed eyes.
Let her step off the ledge as if
          beneath each scapula
          she feels the itch of wings.
Let the sky that cannot hold her
          take her shoes
          but nothing more.
Let mercy turn each pedestrian gaze
          toward the swizzle of white
          that precedes her.
Let glass & steel become

her catafalque.
Let her rest like a beautiful lie.
Let we who did not know her
      be absolved for finding beauty
      in such broken truth—
      for, having looked upon her,
      being powerless to turn away.

The Central Story

after the painting by Magritte

"Everything we see hides another thing, we always want
to see what is hidden by what we see."
  –**René Magritte**

The brown suitcase, locked and set before her
on a table grey as surgical steel,
might contain a secret she keeps
coiled tight as a fiddlehead,
might conceal a loss she cannot bear,
or else it holds the mouth of the river
into which she will wade
until that brief wound heals above her,
until the mud locks her ankles
against all rising.

The tuba could be the curve of a woman's
hip smoothed beneath her lover's palm,
could be progenerative, or maybe
what it means to be made for breath
but to be left breathless all the same.

Her left hand, pressed as it is
against the thick reed of her throat,
is most likely suicidal, unless it is
autoerotic, a declaration of self-censure,
or perhaps a gesture she signs to mean:
Please never speak of me again.

The cerulean behind her is the same
river held restless in the suitcase,
or it is the immutable sky that will be
just the same after she is gone,
or else it is the blue of a lame cliché

for the fog through which she stumbles
along the path that has always led to the water.

And the simple russet dress is the earth
that will cradle her once the river
has relinquished its grasp, or it is the color
of all hope lost, or it is nothing more
than a simple russet dress.

The white cloth might be the way
she feels invisible, or it is the tracery
of a skull that drifts like a cumulus cloud
above the river that is also the sky,
or else it is the nightgown that will
leave her naked below the waist
when she is dragged onto the mossy bank,
the night-shroud that will tangle
and obscure her face from the wild eyes
of her oldest son who is still just a boy,
or else it is the canvas upon which
he will spend the rest of his life in a fury
of trying to draw her back to that last brief
kiss, to the moment she turned, just beyond
the rusted back gate, and regarded him
the way a woman might look at an heirloom
she can no longer keep.

What difference if it didn't happen that way?

Waiting for Houdini's Ghost

Hollywood: 31 October 1936

*For ten futile years following his death, Houdini's wife, Bess, held a
séance each Halloween, hoping his ghost would communicate their
agreed-upon code.*

Another year
unravels
from the thinning
spool.
Candlewick.
Mothlight.
Silver spoon.
Another circle
of hands
entwined beneath
a cacophony of
twisted tin horns,
gauzy heads adrift
in sandalwood
smoke.
And words—
trunks full of
mad guesses,
enough to bury
a man alive
or drag him
to the solemn
hush of a river
bottom.
Then Ford's
stolen lines
that nearly
had you sold.

Ten years
is long enough
to keep
one ear to
this world,
the other pressed
to the hereafter,
enough to hold
the breadth
of desire.
Goodnight
Last Night,
the last dying
ember
has lost its light.

The Execution of Mata Hari

Paris: 15 October 1917

Guilty of nothing but taking
pleasure in the company of men,
she opens her mouth only to
paint her lips one final time.
She tightens the lace corset
whose ivory bones
remind her of a lover's hands
strong and needy beneath
each slight breast,
slips on a dusk-grey dress.
Over her smooth calves
she draws silk stockings
soft as a goodnight kiss,
then bends to fasten
each pearl button
on her ankle-high boots.
Finally, a lapis coat
worn like a cape against
October's sudden chill,
a tricorn hat, the color of
deep bruises, atop raven hair
that's just begun to silver.

It's not yet dawn as she enters
the boxy car that idles
outside the prison gate,
a priest, two nuns, and a jailer
her solemn company
on this last ride that winds
to the edge of Vincennes forest

where the shadowed oaks
still hide, beneath their crimson
and gilt brocade, the dead weight
of a thousand slumbering crows.

Out now, across mud that tugs
their shoes, to a crooked limb
that's been set as a stake
to which they mean to bind her,
though she scorns both bond
and blindfold, blows a ruby kiss
toward her executioners
who shift like nervous horses
before her gaze, steady
and untroubled
as the eyes of graven saints.

Nothing left but to let the sabre
drop, catching the day's
first gold in its descent,
a blued-steel semaphore
that commands twelve fingers
to pull hard against cold triggers,
each man praying his is the one
that bears no harm
as eleven bullets blossom
inside the cage of her ribs,
suffusing her heart
with an aching, foreign light.

And the birds, startled
by the clap of rifle-shot,
rise in a clamorous, gunmetal
cloud while spent powder
drifts above the men who bow
their heads against such cowardice
as the woman drops to her knees,
her flesh, even in death, retaining

the grace of a dancer who surrenders
herself to the bright supplication
of fallen leaves and the cool earth
that begs to hold her.

To Lucifer

And you, most beautiful of all god's
angels, formed from the first rib
of sunlight to break the black
breathlessness of space—
what are we to make of your falling
like a star out of heaven,
crushed under the heel of Michael,
the heel of Mary, and made to twist
along on your shingled belly
as if you were less than the dirt
we toss out of our gardens
because it is too heavy
with its freight of clay—
as if it can be blamed for being
what it is, as if the seed of rebellion
had not been planted
behind your amber eyes as, later,
the shame of nakedness would be
gleaned from the flesh of an apple.
The first sin was neither pride nor
disobedience, but the gift
of agency, which granted us choice—
and so you chose, who were our first light.

Taxonomy

Genesis 2:18–22

After a while, the glitter
began to fade, the way
a bright star, regarded full-on,
becomes its own ghost
behind the shuttered eye.

After a while, he couldn't
look past the next in line,
couldn't bear the beastly
swizzle that curved beyond
the perfect wash of sun
that gilded the perfect pasture
in perfect shades of umber.
Horse. Cow. Rat.
Elephant. Monkey. Mole.
And this was merely shorthand
before the dizzy permutations …
family, genus, species.

After a while, the man
named himself *Adam*.
He invented time and shifts
and workloads
so the nameless might not
overtake him like a foreshadowed
throng of lepers chasing
the hem of a dusty robe.

After a while the creatures
grew restless, demanding
their names of Adam who
threw a trepid glance

over his sunburned shoulder
toward the distant golden city
before he whispered,
Eat or be eaten,
and so inscribed the first
coppery illumination
in the book of the dead,
the maimed, and the dying.

After a while, a century
had passed. But even so,
the sentence stood.
He had to crouch, naked
and limp between the legs,
naming, naming, and no creature
that approached, however bright
of eye or soft of pelt, could
stir him from his torpor.

After a while, the last in line
perched upon his outstretched
hand. *Swift,* he pronounced,
more wish than name,
as it took flight in an elegant
arc above him before dipping
its wings toward the city's
eastern gate.

After a while, all the whiles
congealed like blood
in a ragged wound,
and Adam named the ache
that plagued him *loneliness.*
He cried out from his
empty bed, felt a fist
like iron enter his side,
saw a fairer form bloom
from the snapped curve

of his floating rib.
Like him. And not.
He named this partner *Eve.*

And for a while they knew joy,
though soon enough she grew
weary of halcyon days without
surprise, had intercourse
with the diamond-plate serpent
coiled among the waxy leaves
of the Forbidden Tree.
She tasted the fruit
ripe with *knowing,*
felt the nectar run between
her naked breasts
and so gave birth to desire.

After a while, the one who
gave them breath stepped out
from behind his tangle of
rusted machines, the rancid
tubs filled with things
misshapen.
He told them he knew . . .
had pictures to prove it.
He withered the garden
with a single exhalation,
spat a mouthful of curses
and ordered them gone,
though when the angel
swooped down
with his flaming sword,
they'd already taken
what little they had
and vanished,
having rolled
the thing they named *freedom*
across their tongues

and found it sweet.
Like spoonfuls
of milk and honey.

The Lily of Ecuador

St. Mariana of Jesus, 1618–1645

Friday, at last, and the sun drags
toward its apex. She comes away
from the chipped washbasin, the scrubbing
and scrubbing until her skin is scoured
like earth after fire, pure and ready for
the heft of chain around her slender waist,
each link's mouth slightly open
to better bite the skin that will press between.

And over this, a shapeless black dress to hide
the extravagant curves of her woman's form—
as if the angel always beside her might
find himself unable to look away for shame.

She oils the waist-long veil of her sable
hair to give back light for Light,
then climbs into the tapered length
of the box which will one day bear her
back into the dust from which she came.

She has made a pillow of hemp and broken
glass. She has placed a spoonful
of salt upon her tongue. All day she will
implore the sun to consume her. At night,
she will lie beneath the blue breath of moonlight,
metal thorns piercing the scarred bowl
of her head as she turns first left,
then right, as if rocking an unquiet child,
the empty chalice of her hips aching
with hunger both sacred and profane,
to press her hand to the wound

in her bridegroom's side, her mouth to his
beard that drips with blood and gall.

Abstinence has pulled her senses taut
so that even the spider on the sill spinning
its silken deathtrap is not silent enough to escape
her notice, nor the bees beneath the eaves
whose translucent wings fan the gold
of their combs, to say nothing of the lovers
entwined half a mile to the south, whose sighs
fall around her like a dusting of talc, whose
unclothed flesh smolders in the smoky tallow
glow, leaving ghosts of themselves to copulate
on the unwilling stage of her mind.

She considers the dead
her faith has called back from the lip
of paradise: a child crushed beneath
the hooves of an angry mule,
a murdered wife whose corpse was left
to fester two days in the woods
before a pious man dragged it,
already encircled with a halo
of flies, into the damp of her small cell.
She remembers how their presence felt like
vanished things in the way clothes
strung on a line, inhabited by only wind
and sifted light, offer a sort of false life,
and how the lately-dead sucked in air
like blue newborns when she
signed their eyes with crosses.

She ponders the tremors that three years before
ripped great seams through the heart of Ecuador,
how she took a leather whip, opened
furrows in her back like an April field that waits
to be sown until, at last, the pain she bore
caused the vengeful fist of her god to unfurl.

Now, as plague oozes beneath a thousand
rooftops, she offers herself once more.
A dram of bitter almond, for the taste
of sin. A few grains of sand beneath
the lids of her eyes, to guard their custody.
For each boil that melts from a victim's skin,
two more rise up, unwholesome, unseen,
beneath the folds of her charcoal gown.
How sweet is my Love, she whispers,
as her lungs begin to fill with answered prayer,
a dam that breaks, blood thick as honey
stealing her breath a cupful at a time
until she drowns upon the rough straw,
and the room begins to burn
with mid-day light while, all around
her glowing head, untarnished lilies bloom.

Sokushinbutsu

Yamagata Prefecture, Japan

Begin at sunrise
with a handful of stiltgrass,
hazel, and pine nuts.
Near midnight, before you
lie upon the forest floor,
fill your palms with nutmeg
for a repast.
In the hours between, run
until the fire in your chest
extinguishes breath, then walk
until your diminishing legs
will take you no farther.
Sit where you fall—dung heap,
moss bed, or snow-bank.
Repeat this for 1,000 days.

Next, strip off your clothes
as a snake molts its skin.
Let sun or ice flay you.
Let rain spill like quicksilver
over the rising bones
of your back and number your ribs
like mala beads—a sickled mantra
that circles you at the core.
Tear bark from trees or
take their roots for sustenance.
When your tongue grows thick
with thirst almost a madness,
stoop to lap from puddles
carved by deer that passed
beside the river.
Repeat this for 1,000 days.

Now you must be done with eating.
Let nothing pass your lips but
the bitter sap of the lacquer tree,
which will sicken you
nearly unto death, scour you bright
and hollow as a begging bowl.
Be still and feel yourself begin
to petrify from the inside
so that when you stand after
meditation it will be as if to a chorus
of cracked offal and breaking bone.
Repeat this for 1,000 days.

Finally, enter the chamber
you carved in root-thick earth,
a space so small the crescent
of your shoulders spans
from side to side. Settle like a lotus,
the pads of your feet turned up
as the face of a flower that follows the sun.
Permit no final glance at distant clouds
before the stone is set above you,
nor flinch as the bamboo rod stabs
a blaze of light into the black
to siphon air enough for you to keep alive.

Ring the bell at your side
when you hear the forest stir to life
above you;
again when the owls cry each to each,
so the priests who press their ears
against your tomb
will know you are still breathing.

Repeat this until you can no longer
repeat it.

Now the reed will be withdrawn

like a sword yanked
from a grievous wound.
Now the holy men will
fill the gap with dead leaves
and thick resin.
Now they will wait 1,000 days
to open the mouth of your grave
and behold what has become.

You will either glow
with the hard-won polish
of 3,000 agonies, or you will not.
You will be a thing to be praised
or reviled, to be enshrined
in bright robes or covered
with mud and forgotten.
No matter to the blossoms
that scatter their colors without
fanfare. No matter to the stars
that shine without artifice.

Undark

At first it was just a game
to glow in the dark,
double arches on a brow,
a fanciful handlebar swept
above a sweat-damp upper lip,
or eyelids closed to reveal
twin crescents of aquamarine.
Later came surprises
for sweethearts,
incandescent fingernails,
quick flashes of radiant teeth
in a darkened theatre,
full-mooned areolas
and star-dusted décolletage.

Mostly, though, it was just a job.
Long hours bent over tables
or school desks stroking
slender dials with camel hair
brushes dipped in phosphorescent
cups of glue, zinc sulfide, radium powder.
They called it *Undark*,
a potion to drive blackness away,
give light to dim clock faces,
vouchsafe soldiers a way
through skies made clear by the gleam
of their instrument panels.

250 pieces per day. Twenty dollars,
new shoes, and fresh produce
at each week's weary conclusion.
Who would have guessed
every damp kiss
to point a flattened brush
washed poison over soft mucosa,

ignited a Luciferian flame
that burned, blue-green,
into jawbones slowly eaten
to pumice, or the brilliant
slide behind breastbones
toward luminous loops of bowel,
ribboned veins that fed bone
transmuted to something
hollow as the shaft of a feather,
a holocaust of light
to coax anemic gasps from
aching jaws, pale lips
that blossomed tumors
until the inscrutable
Angel of One Last Breath
drifted in to the hospital's
polished corridors.

Nothing left then
but to carry them out
when the sun gave up its ghost,
zipped into bags to steal their light,
shove them deep in the earth
of St. Columba's or Restland,
sealed in lead-lined boxes.
1600 years to half-life.
No rest.
No rest.
The Radium Girls,
dressed in holiday finest,
hold the candles of their bones
against the airless dark,
consumed by a ravenous fire.

Maria Callas's Tapeworm

for Dan Hoyt

She loves
the way he comes
in the sweet tang
of blood & raw flesh,
how he coils inside her,
the way he never says
Enough.

She feels him glide
down her throat,
sanguine & slick as
pleasure.
He kisses her belly-deep,
swallows her sins,
tucks in her waist
like a hard-boned corset,
polishes her eyes
with fever.
He tightens a fist
inside her
like a miscarried child.

He is the ravenous
secret she keeps,
the one who chisels her
skin closer to bone &
buffs it to a pregnant
glow…
though she knows
that light is false as
the moon's,
though she knows

someday he will
waste her
with his desire.
Someday
he will swallow her
whole.

The Astronomer

after the painting by Vermeer

There is a beaten-copper glow in the day's
angle of descent, the inevitable slide toward gloaming.
The young man has pushed aside the table's coverlet
in blue-black waves of disregard—splay of palm,
sickle blade, half-faces of strange fauna.

He leans toward the celestial globe,
fingers what the day's last, burning exhalations
swathe in yellow-gold. Swirl and vortex of sinuous,
star-boned beasts. Perhaps they are nothing
more than articulations of chaos joined
by primitive minds. Or, perhaps, some deity's
brilliant arithmetic that breathed life into the skies.

The astronomer tucks a tangle of auburn hair
behind his ear in one fluid, habitual motion.
Above his head, the casement forges a golden arrow.
Its fiery tip illuminates the pale flesh of his
index finger paused over Cassiopeia.

Soon, the room will be trellised in shadow. Soon,
stars will shiver like water sluiced from uplifted wings.
The astronomer will rise from the darkened table,
stroll under night's cloud-shirred dome.

So much left to wonder at each day's flared
conclusion. *Chance? Order? What manner of
burning alphabet? And deity?* Divider, radial chart,
the astrolabe's glittering arcs, and this figured
geometry wrapped in the calf-scent of vellum.
He fixes a spot on the whorled face of captive sky,
strains for a theory of accident or purpose,

unable to see what his hands already know.
The right, *As above.* The left, *So below.*

Stasis

Rosalia Lombardo, 1918–1920
Capuchin Catacombs, Palermo, Sicily

Nothing so coarse and fumbling
as the rituals of Pharaoh's high priests
with their hooks and blood-stained bowls,
the dreadful drawing out of brain
through nose we name *excerebration*.
Nor would the simple black sleep
of graveyard earth do for his darling Rosalia,
seven days shy of her second birthday,
choked by serous fluid that filled her
scarred lungs so she drowned
on dry land, a mile's remove
from the glint of Sicilian sand.

How could any father countenance
the amplitude of such loss,
all the long days that seemed
assured and spread out
like ripened fruit on a picnic blanket
gusted away
as if by a sudden summer storm?

What remained was stillness
quiet as the star-strewn galaxies,
his unspoken prayer, if not for return
then at least suspension
of such dreadful undoing,
a deal struck with a lesser god
who guided the hands of Alfredo Salafia
toward mad artifice, a new formulary
to perfect a ghostly stasis:
glycerin to keep the flawless

flesh from dwindling to dust;
chloride and zinc sulfate
to harden all that would go slack
and fall away;
formalin and salicylic acid
to hold back those things unseen
that would consume her
from within like slow fire
that chars deep seams of anthracite.

And now, nearly a century has passed
since they tucked her in this slight sarcophagus,
sealed the glass above that placid face
with paraffin and petitions
to her sainted namesake that she might
keep the black watch of the catacombs
beside this child who's become
little more than a weary cliché,
a girl barely past the cries of infancy
who, it seems, might rise at any instant,
slip shyly down the long corridors
of the dead who regard eternity's endless
endlessness from hooks on the ancient walls.

Rosalia, daughter of airless dark,
patron saint of desolate fathers
and unfaltering denial, what should I say
to the woman who kneels dumbstruck
beside me, who does not know
your perfection is fragile
as the glass that guards you,
that your sleep is a delicate deceit
a simple hammer strike would shatter,
unloosing the dogs of decay?

Tell me, when should we stop
letting grief tell us its beautiful lies?

The Recording Angel

Sculpture by Lorado Taft (1923)
Forest Mound Cemetery, Waupun, Wisconsin

The Recording Angel descended with no quill,
no well, nor ink; had written nothing in the book

splayed on her broad lap, a tome held open
like the wings of a dove she meant to lift skyward

in the thunder-clapped moment just before she was
pinioned to stone. The Recording Angel had not inclined

toward the east or the west to eavesdrop on voices
that hummed like a chorus of one-hundred-thousand

honeybees set loose in a field dense with clover.
The Recording Angel had closed her eyes.

She had lifted her chin toward leaves that flickered
above and around her like an exaltation of larks.

She had declared a flagrant dereliction
despite the wrath she'd surely invoke from the one

whose voice shook the polished halls of paradise,
despite the knowledge it would earn for her,

as it had Lot's transfixed and glittering wife,
the cold restraint of a madman's hand.

And whether salt or bronze is of no consequence,
each being the stiff price a woman paid to bear witness—

one who turned from sanctuary to keep watch

with the city she loved, sheathed in flames;

the other who chose this aching blue planet,
who chose *us*, whose tongues proclaim no gospel but desire.

Something About Her Mouth That Makes Us Want To . . .

The face of the CPR training doll was modeled on the death mask of an unidentified young woman who drowned herself in the Seine River in the late 1880s.

Something about her mouth
that makes us want to

kiss it. Though that's too easy.
She is, after all, wholly cliché,
barely a woman, all polished
countenance, flawless as rain,
an eternal gibbous moon
that hides its dark side
in the shadow of our shadow.

Something about her mouth
that makes us want to

lie so she won't stop smiling
when she lets go
of the bridge's balustrade,
vanishes like a bullet into flesh
while mindless water burns her
lungs like swathes of poison
smoke above a flushed horizon.

Something about her mouth
that makes us want to

steal the secret she is surely
keeping, an ephemeral glimpse of
more than just this,
or maybe the simple happiness
that came from knowing
there was nothing more
that could be done.

Something about her mouth
that makes us want to

           part her lips with pleasure
           like Bernini's slack-jawed saint
           whose inviolate heart is ravaged
           by a seraph robed with fire.

Something about her mouth
that makes us want to

           drown her so we can
           press our lips to that quiet
           acquiescence,
           breathe her back to life
           only to kill her again
           and again, though,
           we will remind ourselves,
           it is only with the very best
           intentions.

Elegy Written in Fire

for Tony
Balboa Park, San Diego

In my dream, it's not a flask of gasoline you press to your scarred chest,
only a favorite book left to ride the steady swell and fall of your breathing

as you drowse between the ancient fig's waterfall roots. When you rise,
it's not because the flint's been struck and it's too late to take it back,

it's merely that you choose to move toward the wind-chopped bay
where the Coronado arcs between the bedrock of two extravagant, glittering shores.

And in my dream, it's only a swarm of midsummer insects that engulf your head,
make you wave your arms as you stumble beneath the scrim of contrails

carved into the Egyptian blue of the night that's swiftly dying.
But my dream never believes its own lies. When I turn away, it makes me

watch you in the silvered face of a rain puddle that can't undo a single thing,
that can only invert the black clouds and billowed gold that shadow you

like infernal heraldry as you try to outpace the terrible, bright thing you are
becoming. And after, when you've gone quiet and the birds have recommenced

their morning song, there will be no one who can name you until, weeks later,
in a too-bright lab, you must say it yourself in the swizzled language of DNA,

though even then they'll get it wrong, really, because if there is any god,
he sometimes makes mistakes that force us to close our lips around gunmetal,

or flick a thumb over the cogged wheel of a cheap plastic lighter
to make the world we cannot bear a moment longer . . .

stop.

Of course I forgive you. *My Falling Star. My Icarus. My Unquenchable.*

Museum of the Holy Souls in Purgatory

Church of the Sacred Heart of Suffrage, Rome

Granted brief reprieve from expiation,
what form might these souls have put on to move,
once again, among the living?
I say, "Sweltering exhalations of wind out of season."
You answer, "Shadows woven from cinder and ash."

It's no matter to the vanishing host of faithful
who wander these crumbling lanes
like a lost tribe in search of something to sustain them,
to hold up to tourists and lovers as blistering proof,
like the singed relics in this small museum
tucked behind the gilded altar of the Sacred Heart,
a room no larger than a prison cell
where fifteen mismatched frames depend
at fevered angles, each smoky pane holding fast
the scorched testament of the almost-saved
who came back to this world speaking a language of fire.

Behold, a husband's nightcap scorched by
the slim gold ring of his burning bride;
a young nun's pale cape gone black at the hem
clutched by her late confessor's hand;
a well-worn psalter pressed tight to a flaming breast—
each earthly artifact a caveat, or so we're told,
from heaven's igneous stepping stone.

But what can the dead tell us that we don't already know?
We are born from water into fire, and beyond
our last breath lies understanding or oblivion.

Love, if the dead go on, they still burn as we do.
So let's light a candle to hold back the vaulted black
beyond this charred assemblage.
Let our prayer be my hand against your cheek,
a long kiss in this chill room, then one more
before we step back into Rome's falling umber,
the ghost of your lips still warm on my mouth.

Swallow

Spring again, and outside our hotel window swallows raise
their raucous cries between branches that bear only
the faintest blush of jade. I watch you, still lost to dreams,
a knife-edge of sun slicing the length of your perfect neck,
and I'm back to yesterday, to the Mutter's two dwarfed
galleries, their brass and polished cases hung with human grief:
a young man's throat flayed and pinned wide to unveil
the tumor that finally choked back his last breath;
twins molded pelvis-to-face in a grotesque parody
of pleasure; the toothless woman, mouth agape,
whose corpulence turned her to soap inside her grave;
countless rows of yellowed bone eaten to lace by syphilis,
and varnished drawers filled with objects swallowed
then later retrieved—dental work, buttons, children's toys,
and a puzzling host of unclasped safety pins.
We passed an hour or more amongst the wreckage of
so much flesh. Long enough to remind me
why I don't have faith in any god. Long enough
to make the lovers who moved ahead of us press
so close I knew their night would end sooner
than most in the comfort of their rumpled bed.
What better salve for sadness than such bliss?
And we, having had our fill of things unsound, stepped back
into the street where the seemingly-whole wrapped their coats
against early evening's chill and carried themselves to the places
strangers go while we drifted, arm in arm, back to the hotel
where you opened your thighs, luminous as x-rays
in the fallen light, and I swallowed the damp gathered there,
then entered you as a swimmer enters a warm, solemn lake.
And we slept, limbs entwined, while the Milk Moon moved
across the sky until morning swallowed it whole, just like
the light that vanishes halfway down the throat
of that nearly-bottomless cave in Mexico where swallows rise
in unison each dawn, unspooling from darkness in a fluttering iris,
until, at last, they spill into daybreak and disappear

toward the far horizon. I think their swift ancestors
must have mesmerized Cortes and his men, made them
draw back their reins and watch a while in wonder. I want
to believe the sight of those thousand-thousand wings lifting as one
made the soldiers stay their torches a heartbeat or more before
they wicked the forest into a second sun to burn their way back
into paradise. And I want to believe they wept to see those birds chase
cinders they mistook for prey until their flight became a smolder,
then a stillness, as they fell back to this earth which, however broken,
beckons us to drink deep. Swallow. Deeper still.

NOTES

Caritas Romana: "Roman Charity" is a term attributed to the Roman historian Valerius Maximus who recorded the tale of a woman named Pero. According to Maximus, Pero's father, Cimon, had been imprisoned and sentenced to death by starvation. Unwilling to allow her father to perish, Pero visited him in his cell and secretly breastfed him. When the jailers discovered what she had done, they were moved to pity and released him.

Litany of "The Most Beautiful Suicide": Based on Robert C. Wiles' iconic photograph of Evelyn McHale.

Mercy: The subtropical region located 30° north and south of the equator is subject to weather conditions that tend to create particularly calm waters. In the past, it was not uncommon for sailing ships to get stranded . . . sometimes for days or weeks. According to legend, crews weakened by lack of food, and running low on drinking water, would sometimes resort to throwing their horses overboard to conserve supplies as well as take advantage of what little wind was present. For this reason, the region is sometimes referred to as "the horse latitudes."

ACKNOWLEDGMENTS

Asheville Poetry Review: "Elegy Written in Fire"

Atlanta Review: "Litany of 'The Most Beautiful Suicide'"

Briar Cliff Review: "If There is Such a Thing as Mercy"

Catamaran: "Cephalophores," "Dog / Buddha," "Falling," "The Central Story"

Chagrin River Review: "The Left Hand of the Devil," "Until the End of the World"

Chariton Review: "Plunder"

Crab Orchard Review: "The Drowned Church of Potosí, Venezuela"

Comstock Review: "Armageddon"

Ekphrasis: "The Astronomer"

Gettysburg Review: "Laika," "The Lily of Ecuador"

Green Briar Review: "The End of All Flight"

Hayden's Ferry Review: "Mercy," "To Lucifer"

Hunger Mountain: "Descent"

I-70 Review: "The Recording Angel," "Waiting for Houdini's Ghost"

Lake Effect: "Caritas Romana," "Swallow," "The Burning of Giordano Bruno," "The Execution of Mata Hari"

North American Review: "Maria Callas's Tapeworm"

Orchard Street Press, Ltd.: "Edison's Last Breath"

World Literature Today: "52," "Museum of the Holy Souls in Purgatory," "Taxonomy"

I'm grateful to my friends, Nickole Brown and Jessica Jacobs, madly talented poets and all-around amazing women, whose home library (which contained hers-and-hers copies of my first two books) played an inadvertent but absolutely crucial role in the publication of this book. Without both of you, Luke Hankins may never have come across my work, and *Obscura* would not have the distinction of bearing Orison's imprint.

And, yes, my heartfelt gratitude to Luke Hankins for your faith in my poems, keen insights, perceptive edits, and selfless devotion of time and effort to make this book the best it could possibly be.

Thanks, too, to Oliver de la Paz and Kathy Fagan, who so kindly and enthusiastically read this manuscript and offered thoughtful remarks. You're both poets I deeply admire, and it's a dream come true to have your superb endorsements.

I'm also grateful to my early readers, friends who consistently pore over and comment on my poems before I ever consider sending them out into the world. I couldn't (and wouldn't) put you in any order but alphabetical: Julie Candela, Carrie Euype, Anthony Imes, Dan Lenk, Mary Barbara Moore, Betty "Lou" O'Brien, and Zack Rogow.

Special thanks to Marsha Huffman: you're one of the best friends of my entire life.

A number of individuals, some of whom I don't even know, donated to make this book possible. Such generosity absolutely humbles me. Regardless of the amount you gave, I offer my deepest gratitude to each and every one of you.

I am indebted to all the editors and readers at journals where some of these poems were originally published, and I extend my thanks even to those who thoughtfully considered, but ultimately turned down, work I submitted. You sacrifice untold hours to the craft of writing and I deeply value and respect your commitment.

Finally, eternal gratitude to my twin, and most-assuredly better half, Gerrie Paino. You were by my side in the womb and will be with me to the tomb. You're my first and best reader, and the most special person in my life. I can't imagine this world without you in it.

ABOUT THE AUTHOR

Frank Paino's first two volumes of poetry were published by Cleveland State University Press: *The Rapture of Matter* (1991) and *Out of Eden* (1997). He has received a number of awards for his work, including a 2016 Individual Excellence Award from The Ohio Arts Council, a Pushcart Prize, and The Cleveland Arts Prize in Literature. His poems have appeared in *Antioch Review, Catamaran, Crazyhorse, The Gettysburg Review, Green Mountains Review, The Kenyon Review, North American Review, Prairie Schooner, Quarterly West,* and *World Literature Today*, among other places.

ABOUT ORISON BOOKS

Orison Books is a 501(c)3 non-profit literary press focused on the life of the spirit from a broad and inclusive range of perspectives. We seek to publish books of exceptional poetry, fiction, and non-fiction from perspectives spanning the spectrum of spiritual and religious thought, ethnicity, gender identity, and sexual orientation.

As a non-profit literary press, Orison Books depends on the support of donors. To find out more about our mission and our books, or to make a donation, please visit www.orisonbooks.com.

Orison Books wishes to thank the following donors, who made
the publication of this book possible.

Laure-Ann Bosselaar
Lurline Brotherson
Nickole Brown & Jessica Jacobs
Donald Butchko
Julie Candela
Jody Cothey
Bernadette Cullen
Yvonne D. Deyling
Michael Dolzani & Stacey Clemence
Patrick Donnelly
Sheila Drain
Veronica Drdek
Carrie Euype & Dan Lenk
Catherine Frances & Rosa Lane
Jessica Griffith
Theodore Harakas
Marie Harris
Marsha Huffman
Anthony Imes

Alana Jochum
Brandon Kucharek
Ed Madden
Mary Barbara Moore
Ladonna Norris
Betty "Lou" O'Brien
Debbie Paino
Gerrie Paino
Lal Shahbaz Qalandar
Barbara Roether
Zack Rogow
Catherine Segurson
Katherine Soniat
Emily Stoddard
Alex Strazzanti
Adrian Tam
Marc Vincent & Alex Nalbach
Malcolm Watson
Francine Witte

For information about supporting upcoming Orison Books titles, please visit www.orisonbooks.com/donate/, or write to Luke Hankins at editor@orisonbooks.com.